Author
John Grisewood

Editor
Angela Crawley

Designer
Rachael Stone

Project Management
Raje Airey

Artwork commissioned by
Susanne Bull

Photography
Patrick Spillane

Photographic Co-ordinator
Leslie Bermingham

Editorial Assistant
Jenni Cozens

Additional editorial help from
Ian Paulyn and Sean Connolly

Editorial Director
Paula Borton

Cover Design
David West • Children's Books

This is a Dempsey Parr Book
This edition published in 2000

Dempsey Parr is an imprint of Parragon
Parragon
Queen Street House
4 Queen Street
Bath BA1 1HE, UK

Copyright © Parragon 1998

Produced by Miles Kelly Publishing Ltd
11, Bardfield Centre, Great Bardfield, Essex CM7 4SL

British Library Cataloguing-in-Publication Data

A catalogue record for this book is available from the British Library.

ISBN 1-84084-781-6

Printed in Hong Kong

First ATLAS

DP

DEMPSEY
PARR

Introduction
Earth Facts

The world we live in is a planet, a huge ball of rock which flies through space. It is called Earth. The Earth travels around our local star, which is called the Sun. As it travels, it spins around and around. It stays on course because it is pulled toward the Sun by a force called gravity. The Earth is one of nine planets that circle the Sun. It is also the only planet on which living things are known to exist.

When we see pictures of Earth taken from out in space, it looks beautiful. We can see the bright blue of the oceans. We can see the brown of the rocks and soil that make up big areas of land. These are called continents. We can see swirling white patterns, too. These are clouds, made up of tiny drops of water. They float in the air that surrounds the planet. Air and water make it possible for us to live on Earth.

Deserts are very dry areas of rock, stones, or sand. This desert is part of **Death Valley**, in California.

High mountain ranges are covered by snow and ice. These are the **Andes** mountains, in South America.

The giant clam is one of the fascinating and varied sorts of sea life found on the **Great Barrier Reef**, off the coast of Queensland in Australia.

4

What is a map?

A map is a plan showing the planet's surface. The Earth's surface is curved, so it can only be shown properly on a round globe. Maps are normally on paper, and so the surface has to be shown as if it were flat.

Many maps show the lie of the land. You can see which areas are low and which are high. You can pick out mountain peaks, coasts and rivers, lakes and seas. These are called natural features. Some maps just show the borders of countries, states, and provinces. Some show cities, roads, and railroad lines. The maps in this atlas show the land and coastlines as well as national borders and cities.

Read the map
This map is of Japan. What are the names of the four main islands? Is the land mostly flat or mountainous?

Spot the mountain
Maps use little badges called symbols. A small black triangle means 'mountain'. Look for the name of the peak and its height in feet above sea level. Other symbols are shown below.

Towns and cities
Towns and cities are shown by round dots. Each country's chief city, or capital, is shown by a square.

JAPAN

HOKKAIDO

Kuril Is. Russia

Asahi Mt. 7,511 ft

Sapporo

Kitakami

Sendai

HONSHU **Tokyo**

Mito

Kyoto Nagoya

Yokohama

Kobe Osaka

Mt. Fuji 12,385 ft

Hiroshima

Kitakyushu

Fukuoka

SHIKOKU

Kii Channel

PACIFIC OCEAN

KYUSHU

Where in the world?
Look for the little round maps to see just where each map fits on to the globe as a whole

Key to symbols
capital city   ■
city or town   ●
mountain   ▲
national border ——
coastline
river
lake
highlands
plains

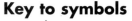

5

Countries of the World

Bolivian women come into market, high in the Andes mountains of South America.

There are 192 countries in the world that are called independent. That means that they rule themselves. Many other lands are called dependencies or colonies, which means that they are ruled by other countries. The number of countries changes all the time, as some split up or else join together to make new nations. The world's biggest country is the Russian Federation, and the world's smallest is Vatican City, which fits inside Rome, the capital of Italy. The country with the most people is China. Nobody at all lives in Antarctica, apart from a few visiting scientists, but several countries claim parts of this land.

The ancestors of the **Araucanian peoples** lived in Chile long before their land was invaded by Europeans.

GREENLAND

Baffin Bay

Chukchi Sea

Beaufort Sea

Bering Strait

Davis Strait

Denmark Strait

ICELA

Hudson Bay

Gulf of Alaska

ALEUTIAN ISLANDS

CANADA

Newfoundland

NORTH

ATLANTIC

OCEAN

PO

UNITED STATES OF AMERICA

CANAR ISLANDS
WES
SA

HAWAIIAN ISLANDS

Gulf of Mexico

BAHAMAS

CUBA

DOMINICAN REPUBLIC

MAUR

MEXICO

W
E
S
T
I
N
D
I
E
S

JAMAICA HAITI

PUERTO RICO

BELIZE

Caribbean Sea

SENE

GUATEMALA HONDURAS

GAMBIA
GUINEA-BISS

EL SALVADOR NICARAGUA

COSTA RICA

TRINIDAD & TOBAGO

SIERRA

PANAMA VENEZUELA

GUYANA

SURINAM

FRENCH GUIANA

COLOMBIA ECUADOR

GALAPAGOS ISLANDS

S O

ATL

O C

PERU

BRAZIL

BOLIVIA

PARAGUAY

CHILE

URUGUAY

ARGENTINA

FALKLAND/MALVINAS ISLANDS

South Georgia

North Americans like to show off their **cowboy** skills at shows called rodeos.

Over 150 different peoples live in the **Russian Federation**. Many have their own languages and way of life.

A father holds his son at **Lijiang**, a town in the mountainous part of Yunnan province, southwest China.

SVALBARD

ZEMLYA FRANTSA IOSIFA

SEVERNAYA ZEMLYA

Novaya Zemlya

Barents Sea

Kara Sea

Laptev Sea

NOVOSIBIRSKIYE OSTROVO

East Siberian Sea

egian a

SWEDEN   FINLAND

NORWAY

Sea of Okhotsk

Bering Sea

ESTONIA

LATVIA

Baltic Sea   LITHUANIA

DENMARK   RUSSIA

RLANDS   BELARUS

MBOURG   GERMANY   POLAND

CZECH

REP. SLOVAKIA   UKRAINE

AUSTRIA

RLAND   HUNGARY   MOLDOVA

CE   SLOVENIA   ROMANIA

CROATIA

RA   SNIA-HERZEGOVINA   YUGOSLAVIA   Black Sea

BULGARIA

ITALY MACEDONIA

ALBANIA   GEORGIA

GREECE   ARMENIA   AZERBAIJAN

TURKEY

Caspian Sea

KAZAKHSTAN

Ara

KYRGYZSTAN

UZBEKISTAN

TURKMENISTAN   TAJIKISTAN

MONGOLIA

RUSSIA

NORTH KOREA   Sea of Japan

SOUTH KOREA   JAPAN

Yellow Sea

CHINA

East China Sea

CYPRUS   SYRIA

TUNISIA   Mediterranean Sea

LEBANON

ISRAEL   IRAQ   IRAN   AFGHANISTAN

JORDAN

A   LIBYA   EGYPT   Red Sea   SAUDI ARABIA QATAR

UNITED ARAB EMIRATES

OMAN

PAKISTAN

NEPAL   BHUTAN

BANGLADESH

BURMA

INDIA

LAOS

TAIWAN

HONG KONG

Philippine Sea

NIGER   CHAD   ERITREA YEMEN

SUDAN   Gulf of Aden

Bay of Bengal

THAILAND   VIETNAM

CAMBODIA   South China Sea

PHILIPPINES

Movement, color and costume are all part of traditional dance in **India**.

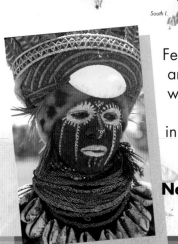

NIGERIA

CENTRAL AFRICAN REPUBLIC   ETHIOPIA

CAMEROON   SOMALIA

ATORIAL   UINEA   CONGO ZAIRE UGANDA KENYA

GABON

RWANDA

BURUNDI

TANZANIA

SRI LANKA

BRUNEI   Celebes Sea

MALAYSIA

EAST   INDIES

MELANESIA

INDONESIA   PAPUA NEW GUINEA

SOLOMON ISLANDS

ANGOLA   MALAWI

ZAMBIA

MOZAMBIQUE

Mozambique Channel

NAMIBIA   ZIMBABWE   MADAGASCAR   MAURITIUS

BOTSWANA   RÉUNION

INDIAN OCEAN

Coral Sea

VANUATU   FIJI

NEW CALEDONIA

SWAZILAND

LESOTHO

SOUTH AFRICA

AUSTRALIA

Tasman Sea

North I.

NEW ZEALAND

South I.

The **Masai** people live on the hot, dusty grasslands of East Africa. The men wear cloaks. The women wear wide collars made of beads.

Feathers, paint, and shells are worn for local festivals in the hills and forests of **Papua New Guinea**.

7

Scandinavia and Finland

These soldiers are on duty outside **Amalienborg Castle** in **Denmark**. Their job is to guard the life of the Danish queen.

RUSSIA

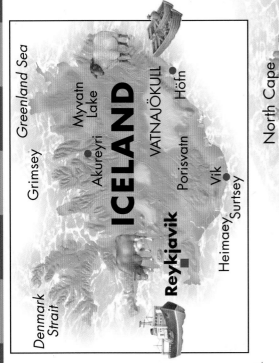

The Baltic and the North Sea are divided by two long arms of the European mainland, which together are known as Scandinavia. The southern arm is called Jutland. Along with several large islands it makes up a country called Denmark. This land is flat and green. Its farms produce butter and bacon.

The other long arm of land stretches down from the Arctic. Its coastline is ragged, with deep sea inlets called fjords in the west. Mountains run down from north to south. There are big forests and thousands of lakes, sparkling blue in summer, but frozen over during the harsh northern winter. The western lands belong to Norway and the eastern lands to Sweden. Oil is taken from beneath the North Sea, metals from the land, and timber from the forests. The eastern shores of the Baltic Sea are taken up by Finland, a land of forests and lakes stretching to the borders of Russia.

FINLAND

Kuopio

Tampere

Helsinki

Turku

Pleasure boats are tied up at a pier on the **Aura river in Turku**. This city is a busy seaport on the Gulf of Bothnia, in southern Finland. It was once the capital of the country, but today the chief city is Helsinki, to the east.

B A L T I C   S E A

Gulf of Bothnia

ÅLAND

SWEDEN

Uppsala

Stockholm

Linköping

GOTLAND

Västervik

Vättern

ÖLAND

Jönköping

Vänern

Bornholm

Göteborg

NORWAY

Trondheim

Bergen

▲ Galdhøpiggen
8,098 ft

Oslo

Stavanger

S k a g e r r

Kattegat

DENMARK

Århus

Copenhagen

Horsens

Malmö

GERMANY

Many Scandinavian fairy tales are about **trolls**. These strange creatures are said to be giants or dwarfs, who live in caves.

The **Saami people** live in the far north, in a region called Lapland. They keep herds of reindeer. This woman is weaving cloth.

Low Countries

The Netherlands and Belgium border the North Sea and are very low lying. For hundreds of years the people there have fought against floods and storms. They have learned to fill in coastal areas to make new farmland, called polder.

The lands near the coast are flat and green, drained by canals and by great rivers such as the Rhine, the Schelde, and the Meuse. Windmills were once used to pump out the wet fields, and may still be seen today. In southern Belgium the land rises to a chain of wooded hills called the Ardennes. These stretch southward into Luxembourg, a tiny country with rich farmland.

The Netherlands is famous for its cheeses, its vegetables, cut flowers, and electrical goods. Belgium produces steel and machinery. Luxembourg produces wine and is a center of business.

The lowlands region is home to several peoples, including Frisians, Dutch, Flemings, and Walloons.

This is the **Atomium**, a strange-looking landmark in Brussels, the capital of Belgium. It was built forty years ago for a big international fair.

Alkmaar is a town in the North Holland region of the Netherlands. Tourists like to visit its famous **cheese market**, and watch the big, round cheeses being carried out and weighed.

Amsterdam, the capital of the Netherlands, is built around a network of canals. The Prinsengracht runs through the old part of the city, which was built in the 1600s.

NETHERLANDS

Groningen

IJsselmeer

West Frisian Islands

Waddenzee

Enschede

Haarlem ■ **Amsterdam**

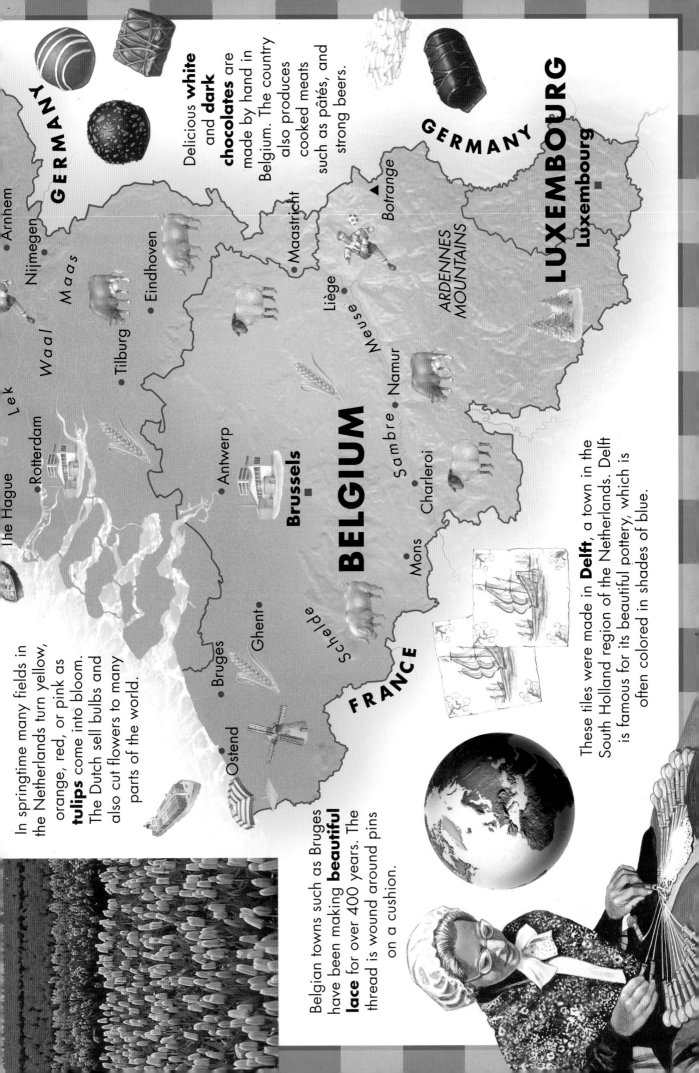

GERMANY

Delicious **white** and **dark** **chocolates** are made by hand in Belgium. The country also produces cooked meats such as pâtés, and strong beers.

GERMANY

LUXEMBOURG
Luxembourg

Arnhem

Nijmegen

Maas

Eindhoven

▲ Maastricht

Botrange ▲

Liège

Meuse

ARDENNES MOUNTAINS

Tilburg

Waal

Lek

The Hague

Rotterdam

Antwerp

Brussels ■

BELGIUM

Sambre Namur

Charleroi

Mons

Schelde

Ghent•

Bruges

Ostend

FRANCE

In springtime many fields in the Netherlands turn yellow, orange, red, or pink as **tulips** come into bloom. The Dutch sell bulbs and also cut flowers to many parts of the world.

Belgian towns such as Bruges have been making **beautiful lace** for over 400 years. The thread is wound around pins on a cushion.

These tiles were made in **Delft**, a town in the South Holland region of the Netherlands. Delft is famous for its beautiful pottery, which is often colored in shades of blue.

British Isles

The British Isles lie off the mainland of Europe. Ocean currents and winds keep the weather mild and moist. The largest island is Great Britain, which is made up of three countries joined together in a United Kingdom. These are England, Scotland and Wales. The second biggest island is called Ireland. The northern part of this is governed as part of the United Kingdom, but most of it is a separate country called the Republic of Ireland.

England has rich farmland in the south and bleak moors in the north. Both Scotland and Wales include highlands where sheep or cattle are raised. Many islands lie to the west and to the north of Scotland. There are many large cities in Great Britain. The biggest of all is London, on the River Thames. The Irish capital is called Dublin. Ireland is a land of green fields, peat bogs, mountains and rivers.

Bagpipes are played in the highlands of Scotland. Pipe music can be sad or stirring. Bagpipes are sometimes used by pop bands as well as by traditional pipers.

This brightly painted **longboat** is on the River Wey, in the southeast of England. Longboats like these were once used to transport pottery and other factory goods. Today they are mostly used for holiday cruises.

SHETLAND ISLANDS

ORKNEY ISLANDS

John o'Groats

NORTH SEA

Peterhead

Aberdeen

Inverness

Dundee

Loch Ness

Perth

NORTH WEST

Forth

Glasgow • Edinburgh

Mallaig

Ben Nevis 1,343 m

SCOTLAND

Ayr

Skye

Lewis

OUTER HEBRIDES

INNER HEBRIDES

Islay

Newcastle

ENGLAND

IRELAND

IRELAND

OCEAN

Isle of Man

IRISH SEA

Dublin

Limerick

Killarney • Cork

Waterford

Norwich

Kingston upon Hull

LINCOLN WOLDS

Leeds

Blackpool

Manchester

Sheffield

Morecambe

Liverpool

CAMBRIAN

WALES

Swansea

Cardiff

Birmingham Coventry

Severn

Bristol

EXMOOR

Oxford

Reading

London

Thames

Chelmsford

Southend-on-Sea
Canterbury

Dover

Brighton

Isle of Wight

Southampton

Exeter

Plymouth

Penzance

ISLES OF SCILLY

ENGLISH CHANNEL

CHANNEL ISLANDS

Green farmland fringes moors, forests and mountains in the **Brecon Beacons National Park**, in Wales.

Lobster pots are piled up on the quay at Dingle, alongside fishing boats. Ireland's Atlantic coast has small islands, peaceful rivers and high cliffs pounded by the ocean.

France and Monaco

France lies at the center of western Europe. It is bordered by the Atlantic Ocean in the west and the Mediterranean Sea in the south. Two high mountain ranges, the Pyrenees and the Alps, divide France from Spain and Italy. In the north, a train tunnel beneath the Channel links the country to England.

The north of the country is mostly flat farmland. The River Seine flows through the French capital, Paris. To the south are the highlands of the Massif Central and the broad valley of the River Rhône.

French farmers grow apples and pears and make all sorts of cheeses. French wines and French cooking too are famous around the world. France makes cars and trains and fashionable clothes.

Monaco is a tiny country on the Mediterranean coast, famous for its gambling and motor racing.

One of the best ways of seeing Paris is by taking a boat trip on the **River Seine**. The city has fine cathedrals and churches, art galleries and museums, bars, and restaurants.

CORSICA
- Ajaccio
- Bonifacio

The **Eiffel Tower** soars above the center of Paris. It was built more than a hundred years ago.

Cherbourg

Le Havre

CHANNEL
ISLANDS (UK)
St.-Malo

Brest

Le Mans

L o i r e

St. Nazaire

Tour

Nantes

Chatellera

Poiters

F R

Cognac

BAY OF
BISCAY)

Bordeaux

Garon

Biarritz

Lourdes

SPAIN

Vines are being pruned in Alsace, a part of France that borders Germany. French grapes produce some of the world's best wines.

Calais
Boulogne
Lille
BELGIUM
LUXEMBOURG GERMANY
ppe
en
tres
Orléans
Reims
Marne
Meuse
Paris
Nancy
Strasbourg
Moselle
Rhine

Haute cuisine means high-quality cooking. French families love to eat well, either at home or in a restatuarant.

mussels
chicken
snails

Saône

SWITZERLAND

N C E

fruit pie

hoges
Clermont-Ferrand
Lyon
Saône
Rhône
Mont Blanc
4,807m

MASSIF
CENTRAL
St.-Étienne
Grenoble
A
L
P
S
ITALY

ogne
Lot
Lot
Rhône

cheese

Avignon

Limoges

ulouse

Montpellier

MONACO
Nice
Cannes

Perpignan
NDORRA

Marseille
Toulon

Many rich people tie up their yachts at **Monte Carlo**, in Monaco. French ports such as Cannes and Nice also attract wealthy tourists.

Germany and the Alps

NORTH SEA

EAST FRISIAN

Three small countries take in most of western Europe's highest mountain range, the Alps. They are Switzerland, Liechtenstein, and Austria. Here, snowy peaks and rivers of ice tower over green valleys, dark forests, and deep lakes. Wooden houses stand in Alpine meadows. They are covered with snow in winter, but are bright with flowers in summer. Languages spoken in the Alps include German, French, Romansh, and Italian.

The Alps stretch northward into southern Germany. Germany is a large country which lies at the heart of Europe. It has forests and steep river valleys, rolling heath, and flat plains. Sandy coasts border the North Sea and the Baltic Sea. Germany has many big cities, with factories producing cars, chemical products, and electrical goods, but it also has pretty villages dating back to the Middle Ages. The German language is spoken throughout, but with many different accents.

The **Matterhorn** is a great needle of rock and ice. It rises in the Swiss Alps, near the Italian border.

Hamb

Bremen

Weser

Hannover

HARZ

Rhine

Dortmund

Essen

Düsseldorf

Cologne (Köln)

Bonn

GERMA

Rhine

Frankfurt am Mai

Stuttgart

FRANCE

Rhine

BLACK FOREST

Lake Consta (Bodensee

Zurich

LIECHTENST

Vaduz

Bern

SWITZERLAND

Lake Geneva

ALPS

Geneva

BALTIC SEA

Berlin is the capital of Germany. It is an exciting, artistic city, but in the last hundred years it has suffered terribly from wars and troubles. This is the **Reichstag**, built a hundred years ago for the German parliament.

Oder

POLAND

Berlin

Elbe

Elbe

Weimar

•Leipzig

•Dresden

NY

CZECH REPUBLIC

emberg
(rnberg)

anube

Munich
(München)

Salzburg

nsbruck

Linz

AUSTRIA

Vienna
Danube

•Graz

SLOVENIA

Lights shine out over the snowy forest at Lech, in **Vorarlberg**, western Austria. The Alpine lands attract walkers in summer and skiers in winter.

Munich is the chief town of Bavaria in southern Germany. During the autumn **Oktoberfest**, tourists join Bavarians in traditional dress to drink big glasses of the local beer.

Kaffee und Küchen—coffee and cakes—are a special treat in Germany and in the cafés of Vienna, the Austrian capital.

Spain and Portugal

The Iberian peninsula is a great block of land which juts out into the Atlantic Ocean. It is ringed by the snowy mountains of the Pyrenees, the Cantabrian ranges, and the Sierra Nevada. Much of it is dry and hot in summer. Rivers cross the western plains and flow into the Atlantic.

The region grows grapes for wine, olives, oranges, and cork. There are large fishing fleets. Factories produce cars and leather goods. Many tourists spend their vacations on the coasts.

There are three nations on the Iberian peninsula. The smallest is Andorra, high in the Pyrenees. Portugal, in the west, is a beautiful country with its own language. The largest country is Spain. Here, Spanish is spoken everywhere, but a number of other peoples have their own languages and way of life, including the Basques, Galicians, and Catalans. A fourth piece of land, Gibraltar in the far south, is a British colony.

Bay of Biscay

La Coruña

Gijón

CANTABRIA

CAPE FINISTERRE

Vigo

Vallado

Porto

Douro

PORTUGAL

Coimbra

Taj

Tagus

Lisbon

Guadiana

Córd

Seville • Guadalqu

Gulf of Cadiz
A thousand years ago, Arab peoples from North Africa ruled most of Spain. They were Muslims and built beautiful **mosques** such as this one in Cordoba.

Cádiz

Gibraltar (U.

Strait of Gibra

Ronda is a small town of white houses in Andalucía, in southern Spain. It is built on the edge of towering cliffs which are linked by high bridges.

FRANCE

PYRENEES

ANDORRA
Andorra la Vella

Bilbao

OUNTAINS

Vitoria

Pamplona

Ebro

Duero

Saragossa

Barcelona

SPAIN

Madrid

Menorca

Mallorca

Palma

Valencia

Ibiza
Ibiza

Spanish girls in traditional costume enjoy all the fun of the fair. Spain has many festivals called **fiestas**. Many of these celebrate Christian saints' days.

Alicante

diana

La Carolina
Linares

Murcia

Granada

MEDITERRANEAN SEA

Portuguese food includes delicious seafood dishes, sardines, fruits, and wines. The drink port takes its name from the town of Oporto.

19

Garda is the largest lake in Italy. It is set among the high peaks of the Alps and has attracted tourists since the days of the ancient Romans.

Carnival is a festival held in the week before the Christian period of Lent. It is a time for parties and fancy dress. In Venice people wear masks and beautiful costumes and cloaks.

SLOVENIA

Trieste

Venice

SAN MARINO
San Marino

ITALY

Vatican City
(in Rome)
Rome

Latina

TYRRHENIAN

Bari

AUSTRIA

SWITZERLAND

Verona

Po

Bologna

Florence

Pisa

ALPS

APENNINES

Milan

Genoa

Turin

MONACO

Corsica (France)

Many famous cars are produced in Italy. They include the fast **Ferrari** sports car and racing cars as well as the Fiat range of family cars.

FRANCE

Italy and its Neighbors

Italy is a long strip of land stretching into the Mediterranean Sea. In the north are the Alps, a range of high mountains. Below these is a wide plain, crossed by the River Po.

The Appenine mountains run down the center of the country. Southern Italy includes large areas of dry scrubland. Volcanoes and earthquakes are common. Italy also includes the islands of Sicily and Sardinia.

Italy is the world's biggest wine producer and also exports many foods, including pasta, sauces, olives, and salami sausages. Factories in the north produce cars, clothes, and leather goods.

Inside Italy there are two other countries, tiny San Marino and also Vatican City, headquarters of the Roman Catholic Church. Another small country, Malta, lies to the south of Sicily.

Pisa is a town on the River Arno, in the Italian region of Tuscany. Medieval buildings around the central square include a cathedral, a building for baptisms and a famous bell tower which leans over sideways!

SARDINIA

Cagliari

LIPARI ISLANDS

Palermo

SICILY

Catania

IONIAN SEA

Fishing boats are moored in the harbor of Valletta, the capital of **MALTA**. **Malta**. This island nation lies to the south of Sicily.

Italy is famous for making some of world's most delicious ice-creams. An ice-cream parlor is called a **gelateria**.

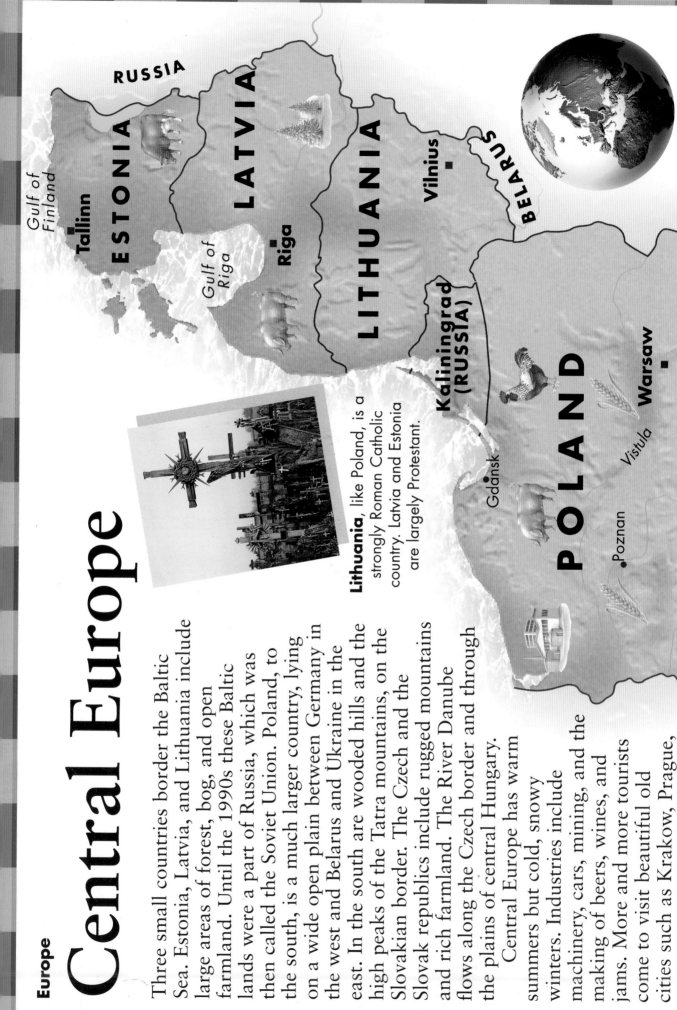

Central Europe

Three small countries border the Baltic Sea. Estonia, Latvia, and Lithuania include large areas of forest, bog, and open farmland. Until the 1990s these Baltic lands were a part of Russia, which was then called the Soviet Union. Poland, to the south, is a much larger country, lying on a wide open plain between Germany in the west and Belarus and Ukraine in the east. In the south are wooded hills and the high peaks of the Tatra mountains, on the Slovakian border. The Czech and the Slovak republics include rugged mountains and rich farmland. The River Danube flows along the Czech border and through the plains of central Hungary.

Central Europe has warm summers but cold, snowy winters. Industries include machinery, cars, mining, and the making of beers, wines, and jams. More and more tourists come to visit beautiful old cities such as Krakow, Prague, and Budapest.

Lithuania, like Poland, is a strongly Roman Catholic country. Latvia and Estonia are largely Protestant.

RUSSIA

Gulf of Finland

Tallinn

ESTONIA

Gulf of Riga

Riga

LATVIA

LITHUANIA

Vilnius

BELARUS

Kaliningrad (RUSSIA)

Gdansk

Poznan

Vistula

Warsaw

POLAND

Shoppers buy vegetables from a **market stall** in Prague. Central European farms produce wheat, potatoes, barley, corn, sugarbeet and sunflowers.

Vistula

Krakow

Wroclaw

GER

Prague

CZECH REPUBLIC

SLOVAK REPUBLIC

Bratislava

AUSTRIA

Budapest

HUNGARY

ROMANIA

More than 1,000 years ago, **Wenceslas** ruled Bohemia, which is now part of the Czech Republic. His statue may be seen in Prague. He is remembered in the words of a Christmas carol, *Good King Wenceslas.*

This fine old **tall ship** is from Poland. It is used for training young sailors. The Baltic Sea has been a center of trade for thousands of years.

These women are wearing **Estonian costume.** Estonia has been ruled by many other countries over the ages, but has managed to keep up its old traditions.

Goulash is a dish that was first made in Hungary. It is a beef stew flavored with spicy red pepper and sour cream.

23

Europe

The son of an Albanian farmer shows off his favorite cow. **Albania** is a small, mountainous country on the Adriatic coast.

It is time to make hay on this **Romanian farm**. Everyone in the family lends a hand. The hay will be fed to the animals during the cold months of winter.

The **Parthenon** is a splendid temple, built in the days of the ancient Greeks. It still towers over Athens, the capital city of Greece.

UKRAINE

Cluj-Napoca

Mureş

Tîrgu Mures

Alba Iulia

ROMAN

HUNGARY

Timisoara

Brasov

Drava

Tisz

Moldoveanu
8,341 ft

Ljubljana

SLOVENIA

Zagreb

CROATIA

Kupa

Osijek

Sava

VOJVODINA

Belgrade

TRANSYLVANIAN ALPS

Buchare

BOSNIA - HERZEGOVINA

Smederevo

Sarajevo

DINARIC

Split

YUGOSLAVIA SERBIA

BALKAN MOUNTAINS

Kam

MONTENEGRO

Dubrovnik Podgorica KOSOVO

Lake Scutari

Sofia Kazanluk

BULGARIA

Stara Zagor

Plovdiv

Skopje

MACEDONIA

Tiranë

ALBANIA

Thessaloníki

Mt Olympus
9,567 ft

Corfu

GREECE

Lesb

AEGEAN
SEA Chio

Ándros

Sá

Athens

Ná

Thíra

Cythera

SEA OF CR

Iráklion Cre

Romania and the Balkans

Romania lies on the Black Sea coast. It is a land of mountains and forests. A large triangle of land stretches southward from Central Europe, ending in chains of islands. It is called the Balkan peninsula and is bordered by the Adriatic, Black, and Aegean Seas. The region has rocky mountain ranges and often suffers from earthquakes. Summers are dry and hot. Winters are very cold in the north, but mild in the south. The region produces timber, wines, olives, fruit, and dairy products.

Bulgaria lies in the northeast of the peninsula. It has large areas of rich farmland. The northwestern Balkan lands used to be part of one big nation called Yugoslavia, but they now make up five different countries. Greece is the southernmost country of the Balkans and includes many islands. Its ancient villages and fine beaches attract many tourists.

churches, whitewashed villages, and blue seas are typical of the Greek lands. This is **Thira**, a volcanic island that is also known as Santorini.

Greek meals might include salad with olives, seafood such as fish or squid, stuffed peppers, beans, a type of wine called retsina, and sweet, sticky pastries such as baklava.

MOUTHS OF THE DANUBE

Constanta

Varna

BLACK SEA

Rhodes

Roses are picked in the Kazanluk region of **Bulgaria**. Their sweet-smelling petals are used to make attar of roses, an oil used in making perfumes.

Zagreb, the capital of **Croatia**, is near the Slovenian border, on the Sava River. The city is on the main route from western Europe to Greece.

Sunflowers are grown as a crop in many parts of the Balkans. Their seeds may be pressed to make vegetable oil or roasted for eating.

Russian Federation

The Russian Federation is the world's biggest country. It stretches across two continents, Europe and Asia. When the sun is rising in Vladivostok, on the Pacific Coast, it is setting on the capital, Moscow. In the Arctic north there is an icy plain, the tundra. To the south of this there are huge forests, the home of brown bears. The countryside also takes in rolling farmland called steppes, deserts, and high mountain ranges. Europe's longest river is the Volga, more than 2,300 miles long, which flows into the Caspian Sea. To the east is Baikal, the deepest lake in the world.

Before 1991 all the countries on this map were part of one huge country called the Soviet Union. After 1991 many of the lands around the Soviet borders broke away to form separate countries. More than a hundred different peoples live in the region, beside the Russians themselves.

St. Basil's Cathedral stands in Red Square, in Moscow.

In the days of the Soviet Union, big statues were put up showing people working hard for their country. These **farmers** are harvesting wheat. It is still an important crop today.

FINLAND

BAREN SEA

Murmansk

Archangel

St Petersburg

BELARUS

Minsk

Moscow

Nizhniy Novgorod

Kazan

UKRAINE

Kiev

Chisinau

MOLDOVA

Don

Volga

Samara

Ural

URAL MOUNTAI

Yekaterin

BLACK SEA

GEORGIA
ARMENIA
AZERBAIJAN

Caspian Sea

KAZAKHSTAN

Aqr

Aral Sea

TURKMENISTAN

Bishke

Ashgabat

Tashkent

Dushar

I R A N

TAJIKISTA

One third of **Armenians** still work on the land. They produce vegetables and fruit or raise sheep and cattle.

Fine **silk** is produced and woven into cloth in the meretia region of Georgia.

In the Middle Ages, Russian monks made beautiful **Bibles** like this one, and painted holy pictures called icons.

Wrangel I.

Franz Josef Land

Severnaya Zemlya

New Siberian Islands

ovaya Zemlya

KARA SEA

KAMCHATKA PENINSULA

EAST SIBERIAN UPLANDS

CENTRAL SIBERIAN PLATEAU

Lena

Yenisey

Yakutsk

RUSSIA

SEA OF OKHOTSK

Sakhalin

Ob

Angara

Amur

Khabarovsk

Sour cream

CHINA

msk

Novosibirsk

Lake Baykal

Irkutsk

Vladivostok

CHINA

Blinis

maty

Beetroot

YRGYZSTAN

Borscht is made from beetroots and served with sour cream and blinis.

27

Canada and Greenland

ARCTIC
OCEAN

Most Canadian towns are in the south, near the United States border, the Great Lakes, or the St. Lawrence River. The north is a wilderness, with frozen plains, vast forests, mountains, and blue lakes. Winters are long and severe, but summers can be mild or warm. Most Canadians are English-speaking, descended from British settlers. A large number are French-speaking, especially in the province of Québec. There are also First Peoples, such as the Innu, Mohawk, Cree, and Micmac. In Arctic Canada are the Inuit people, who traditionally live by hunting seals and polar bears.

Inuit people also live in Greenland, along with descendants of Danish settlers. This is the world's largest island. Its rocky land is covered in a thick sheet of Arctic ice.

BEAUFORT
SEA

Banks Island

Victoria Island

ALASKA (U.S.A.)

MACKENZIE

Mackenzie

Norman Wells

Great Bear
Lake

YUKON
TERRITORY

Whitehorse

Liard

Great Slave Lake

NORTHWEST TERRITOR

R

BRITISH
COLUMBIA

O

C

CAN

QUEEN
CHARLOTTE
ISLANDS

K

ALBERTA

MANIT

Y

SASKATCHEWAN

Calgary

Vancouver
Island

Vancouver

Regina

Win

UNITED STATES OF AME

Maple trees grow colorful leaves in autumn. The maple leaf is a badge of Canada and is shown on the national flag.

Totem poles are still raised outsid villages by the First Peoples of Britis Columbia. They are carved with birds and beasts and figures from myths, legends and family history.

Ellesmere
Island

**GREENLAND
(Denmark)**

The Niagara Falls lie on
the border between
Ontario, Canada, and
the state of New York.
The power of the falling
water is used to make
electricity.

BAFFIN BAY

Baffin Island

*LABRADOR
SEA*

Parts of the **St.
Lawrence** river have
been turned into a
"seaway" or canal.
This allows ships to reach
Lake Ontario from the
Atlantic Ocean.

HUDSON BAY

ADA

NEWFOUNDLAND

St John's

St. Lawrence

PRINCE
EDWARD
ISLAND

ONTARIO   QUEBEC

Quebec   NEW   NOVA SCOTIA
               BRUNSWICK

Lake Superior

Lake Huron   **Ottawa**   Montreal

Toronto   *Lake Ontario*

Niagara Falls   Officers of the Royal
Lake   Canadian Mounted Police
Erie are known as **"Mounties."**
On parade, they wear smart
red jackets and big hats.

The United States of America

The North American **raccoon** is a furry little creature with black patches on its eyes and a ringed tail. It comes out by night.

The United States of America (USA) stretch the whole way from the Atlantic Ocean to the Pacific. There are 50 states in all. They take in woodlands, whose leaves turn red and gold each autumn, and long ranges of hills such as the Appalachians. They include the Great Lakes and the rivers Mississippi and Missouri, which flow into the steamy Gulf of Mexico. There are wide open grasslands called prairies, which are given over to farming and cattle ranching. There is the great Rocky Mountain chain. There are the burning dry deserts of the southwest and the rainy, misty forests of Oregon and Washington State. Two American states are separated from the others. They are Alaska, stretching from Canada into the frozen Arctic, and Hawaii, a group of islands and volcanoes far out in the Pacific Ocean.

CANADA

Seattle
WASHINGTON
CASCADE RANGE
OREGON
IDAHO
Snake
MONTANA
Black Hills
Rapid
WYOMING
Great Salt Lake
Rock Springs
Boulder
NEVADA
UTAH
Denve
GREAT BASIN
Grand Junction
COLORAD
San Francisco
Las Vegas
CALIFORNIA
Grand Canyon
NEW MEXICO
Los Angeles
Colorado
ARIZONA
Rio Grande
San Diego
Phoenix
Douglas
MEXICO

Rainbow Bridge is an arch of pink rock in the state of Utah. Over the ages, wind and water have worn it down into this strange shape.

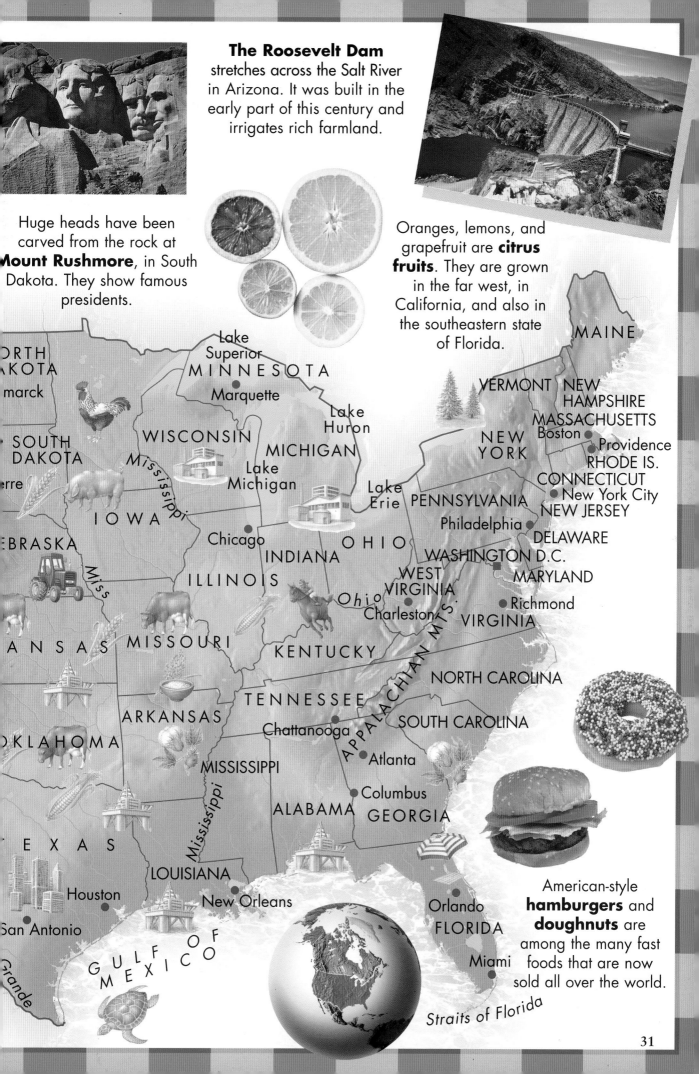

The Roosevelt Dam stretches across the Salt River in Arizona. It was built in the early part of this century and irrigates rich farmland.

Huge heads have been carved from the rock at **Mount Rushmore**, in South Dakota. They show famous presidents.

Oranges, lemons, and grapefruit are **citrus fruits**. They are grown in the far west, in California, and also in the southeastern state of Florida.

American-style **hamburgers** and **doughnuts** are among the many fast foods that are now sold all over the world.

The USA has many big, bustling cities. In the west is San Francisco. It is a beautiful port beside the blue Pacific Ocean. Los Angeles is a huge city full of traffic. A part of it, called Hollywood, is where many famous films have been made. Chicago, on Lake Michigan, was where skyscrapers were first built, more than a hundred years ago. Detroit, on Lake Erie, is where many automobiles are made. And New York City, in the east, is the biggest city of them all. It is nicknamed the Big Apple. The capital of the country is Washington D.C. This is the center of government and is also where the US president lives, in the White House. It isn't in one of the states but in a special district called Columbia.

Many different peoples live in the USA today. Native Americans are descended from the very first people to settle in North America. They include peoples such as the Navajo, Apache, and Cree. Many Americans are descended from European settlers. New

The **World Trade Center** has two tall towers. They rise up from the water's edge on the island of Manhattan. This is right at the center of New York City, one of the largest and busiest cities in the world.

Rattlesnakes live in the hot, dry lands of Texas and the southwest. They are very dangerous. They rattle their tails as a warning before they bite you.

Dance and song make up a **traditional welcome** to the Hawaiian islands. Hawaii's links with the USA go back 100 years.

KAUAI
NIIHAU
OAHU
Honolulu
MOLOKAI
LANAI
MAUI
KAHOOLAWE
HAWAII
Hilo

The USA has many exciting **theme parks**, where children can enjoy fun and fantasy.

The **Californian condor** is very, very rare. It has huge wings, about 10 feet across.

other languages such as Spanish are spoken in some cities. The USA is a country with rich farmland and many mineral mines. Its factories produce computers, cars, drinks and foods, clothing, and all sorts of other goods. It is also a center of the film industry, banking, and business. This has made it one of the world's richest and most powerful countries.

Settlers came from Britain and Ireland, Italy, France, Spain, Greece, Germany, Poland, and the Netherlands. African Americans are the descendants of West Africans who were brought to America hundreds of years ago. Some Americans originally came from Asia, including Jews, Chinese, and Vietnamese. The Hawaiians are Polynesians, one of the Pacific peoples. All these different groups are proud of their background, but they now belong to one big country, the USA. Today most Americans speak English, but

A shuttle is launched into space on the back of huge rockets. It is leaving Cape Canaveral in Florida.

The bright city lights of **Las Vegas** shine out over the desert in the state of Nevada. People come here to gamble, see shows, and stay in hotels.

Mexico, Central America, and the Caribbean

Guacamole

Chillies

Tortillas are cornmeal pancakes made in Central America. They may be served with beans and hot chillies.

Tortillas

Beer

Mexico lies between the Gulf of Mexico and the Pacific Ocean. It is a land of hot deserts, mountain ranges, forests, and sandy beaches. Earthquakes are common and there are volcanoes, too. Mexico City is the country's capital. Once it was the chief city of the Aztec people and called Tenochtitlán. Many great civilizations were started in the region long ago.

To the south of Mexico are the seven small countries of Central America. Panama is crossed by a canal, which links the Atlantic and Pacific Oceans. Spanish is the main language of the region. Many of its

Baja California

SIERRA MADRE

SIERRA MADRE

Rio Grande

Matamoros

Culiacán

Monterrey

GULF OF MEXICO

Havana

CU

Guadalajara

León

Cancún

Cayma
Islands (U

Mexico City

Veracruz

MEXICO

Coatzacoalcas

Belmopan

BELIZE

Acapulco

GUATEMALA

HONDURAS

PACIFIC
OCEAN

Guatemala City

Tegucigalpa

These Native American women from **Guatemala** wear colorful clothes they have woven by hand. Each village has its own patterns and styles.

San Salvador

EL SALVADOR

NICARAGU

Managua

San José

Pana

COSTA RICA

PANA

peoples are descended from the Spanish soldiers who invaded the Americas nearly 500 years ago. Others are descended from Native Americans. Central American crops include corn and bananas.

The Caribbean Sea lies to the east of Central America. It has thousands of islands, the largest of which is Cuba. Caribbean peoples include many whose ancestors came from West Africa. There are also some Caribbeans of Native American, Spanish, French, British, Dutch, and Asian descent. The islands have a warm, tropical climate in which sugarcane and bananas grow well. Hurricanes are common in the later summer and autumn. The islands are famous for their carnivals.

Brilliantly colored **hummingbirds** hover as they sip nectar from flowers. They are found in both Central America and the Caribbean.

Warm blue seas, fine beaches, and watersports attract millions of tourists to the Caribbean islands each year. This is **Barbados**.

How would you like to dive off this cliff into the sea? This is one of the sights to be seen at **Acapulco**, in Mexico.

BAHAMAS

Turks & Caicos Islands (U.K.)

Virgin Is. (U.K. & U.S.)

ANTIGUA & BARBUDA

Puerto Rico (U.S.)

ST. KITTS & NEVIS

Montserrat (U.K.)

Guadeloupe (FR.)

DOMINICA

Martinique (FR.)

HAITI

DOMINICAN REPUBLIC

JAMAICA

ST. LUCIA

CARIBBEAN SEA

ST. VINCENT & THE GRENADINES

BARBADOS

GRENADA

TRINIDAD & TOBAGO

Mexico and parts of Central America have many ancient ruins and statues, like this **warrior** carved from stone. They date back to the ancient civilizations that once grew up here.

Old churches and buildings, like this one in **Costa Rica**, remind us that this region was once ruled by Spain.

The Northern Andes

South America is joined to Central America by a narrow strip of land. To the south, the Andes mountains run all the way down the continent. Their high, snowy peaks divide the hot lands along the coast from the rain forests and great rivers of the east.

Colombia is a beautiful country, which lies across three bands of the Andes range. The rocks are mined for gold and precious green stones called emeralds. Ecuador is named for the Spanish word for Equator. Bananas and sugarcane grow in the warm climate here, and coffee too on the slopes of hills. In Peru, farmers work high in the mountains, growing potatoes, corn and a grain called quinoa. Along the coast fishermen catch tuna and sardines. Bolivia has great forests and tin mines.

About 500 years ago, the Inca people ruled a huge empire in the Andes. It was conquered by Spanish soldiers. Many peoples of the region are descended from Native American peoples and from the Spanish.

This boat is made of reeds, by the **Aymara people.** They live around Lake Titicaca, which is on the border between Peru and Bolivia.

The green turtle lives in the sea along the coasts of Peru, Ecuador, and Colombia. It breeds on lonely, sandy beaches and is becoming very rare.

CARIBBEAN SEA

VENEZUELA

PANAMA

Bogotá

COLOMBIA

Amazon

Iquitos

Quito

ECUADOR

S

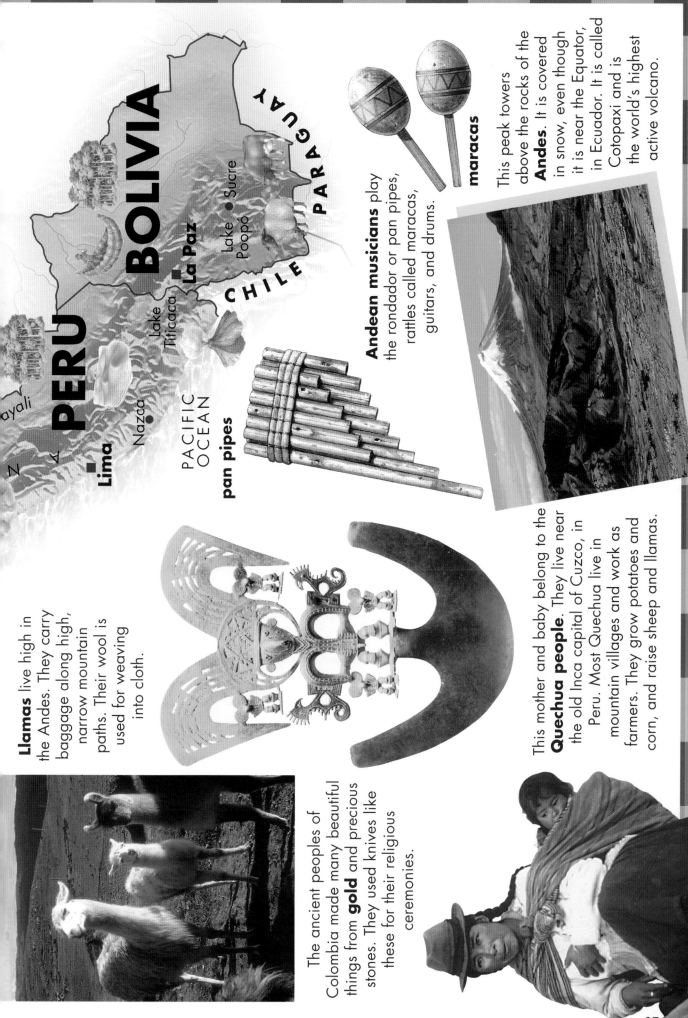

PERU

BOLIVIA

PARAGUAY

CHILE

Lima

Nazca

Lake Titicaca

La Paz

Lake Poopó

Sucre

ayali

PACIFIC OCEAN

pan pipes

Andean musicians play the rondador or pan pipes, rattles called maracas, guitars, and drums.

maracas

This peak towers above the rocks of the **Andes**. It is covered in snow, even though it is near the Equator, in Ecuador. It is called Cotopaxi and is the world's highest active volcano.

Llamas live high in the Andes. They carry baggage along high, narrow mountain paths. Their wool is used for weaving into cloth.

The ancient peoples of Colombia made many beautiful things from **gold** and precious stones. They used knives like these for their religious ceremonies.

This mother and baby belong to the **Quechua people**. They live near the old Inca capital of Cuzco, in Peru. Most Quechua live in mountain villages and work as farmers. They grow potatoes and corn, and raise sheep and llamas.

Brazil and its Neighbors

Carac·

VENEZUEL

Orinoc

COLOMBIA

The **Iguaçu Falls** lie on the border between Brazil and Argentina. The river thunders over hundreds of waterfalls.

Brazil is the biggest country in South America. It is a hot country with grassland, swamps, and dry bush. A large area is covered in rain forest. This is the home of monkeys, brightly colored parrots, and gigantic snakes called anacondas. One of the world's two longest rivers, the Amazon, flows through the forest to the Atlantic Ocean. On the coast there are many big cities. Some city dwellers are rich, but many are very poor.

Venezuela is on the Caribbean coast. It is crossed by another great river called the Orinoco.

A large sea inlet called Lake Maracaibo is the center of Venezuela's oil industry. Three other small countries, called Guyana, Suriname, and French Guiana, lie on the tropical north coast. They produce sugarcane, rice, chilli peppers, and fruits.

This part of South America is home to many different Native American peoples, as well as people descended from Africans and Europeans. The region was once ruled by Portugal, Spain, France, Britain, and the Netherlands.

PERU

This cathedral is in **Brasília**, the capital of Brazil. This modern city was specially built inland, to the south of the great forests.

There are many different kinds of **poison-arrow frog** in South America. Their deadly poison is smeared on arrows and darts by Native American hunters.

This beautiful tropical plant is called the **bird-of-paradise flower**.

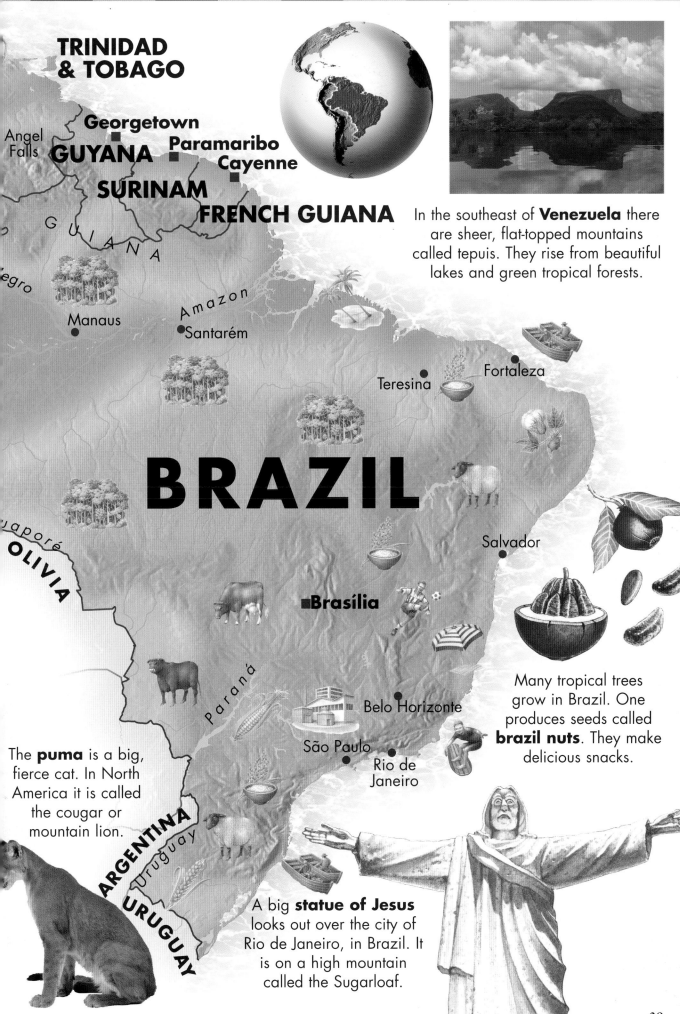

TRINIDAD & TOBAGO

Angel Falls

Georgetown

GUYANA

Paramaribo
Cayenne

SURINAM

FRENCH GUIANA

G U I A N A

egro

Amazon

Manaus

•Santarém

In the southeast of **Venezuela** there are sheer, flat-topped mountains called tepuis. They rise from beautiful lakes and green tropical forests.

Teresina

Fortaleza

BRAZIL

Salvador

aporé

OLIVIA

Paraná

■**Brasília**

Belo Horizonte

São Paulo

Rio de Janeiro

Many tropical trees grow in Brazil. One produces seeds called **brazil nuts**. They make delicious snacks.

The **puma** is a big, fierce cat. In North America it is called the cougar or mountain lion.

ARGENTINA

Uruguay

URUGUAY

A big **statue of Jesus** looks out over the city of Rio de Janeiro, in Brazil. It is on a high mountain called the Sugarloaf.

39

Argentina and its Neighbors

Southern South America is a big triangle of land. The pointed end stretches south toward Antarctica. It breaks up into islands around Tierra del Fuego. Gales whip up huge waves around the southern tip, which is called Cape Horn. As you travel north, you come to the dry, windy valleys of Patagonia, the high Andes mountains, the rich grassland of the Pampas, and the hot, damp Gran Chaco region.

Argentina is a big country, which raises beef cattle and sheep. It borders the Atlantic Ocean. Far offshore are the remote Falkland or Malvinas islands. Uruguay and Paraguay are two small countries to the north, which also raise cattle. Chile, to the west of the Andes, is a long, narrow land. It borders the Pacific Ocean. It has large areas of desert, where it hardly ever rains. It also has warm farmland, where grapes can be grown.

PARAGUAY

Concepción

Asunción

Pilcomayo

Bermejo

Formosa

Corrientes

CHACO

GRAN

Córdoba

Rosario

Buenos Aires

Paraguay

Paraná

PAMPAS

URUGUAY

Montevideo

Negro

ARGENTINA

Santiago

CHILE

Concepción

ATACAMA DESERT

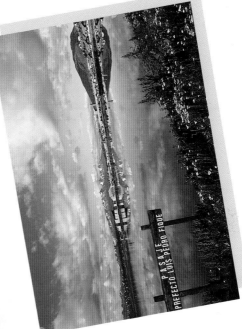

The snow-capped volcano of **Villarrica** rises above a milder landscape near Pucón, in Chile.

The **gauchos** are the cowboys of the Pampas grasslands in Argentina. They are skilled at riding horses and roping cattle. They used to be famous for their wild adventures.

Tomatoes were first grown in South America, on the slopes of the Andes mountains. Today they are grown all over the world.

FALKLAND/MALVINAS ISLANDS

• Stanley

Ushuaia is a port in **Tierra del Fuego**, in the far south of Argentina. The people who live there raise sheep and go fishing.

PACIFIC OCEAN

PATAGO

Tierra del Fuego

Cape Horn

The **rhea** is a large South American bird that can grow to 5 feet tall. It cannot fly and lives on the Pampas.

41

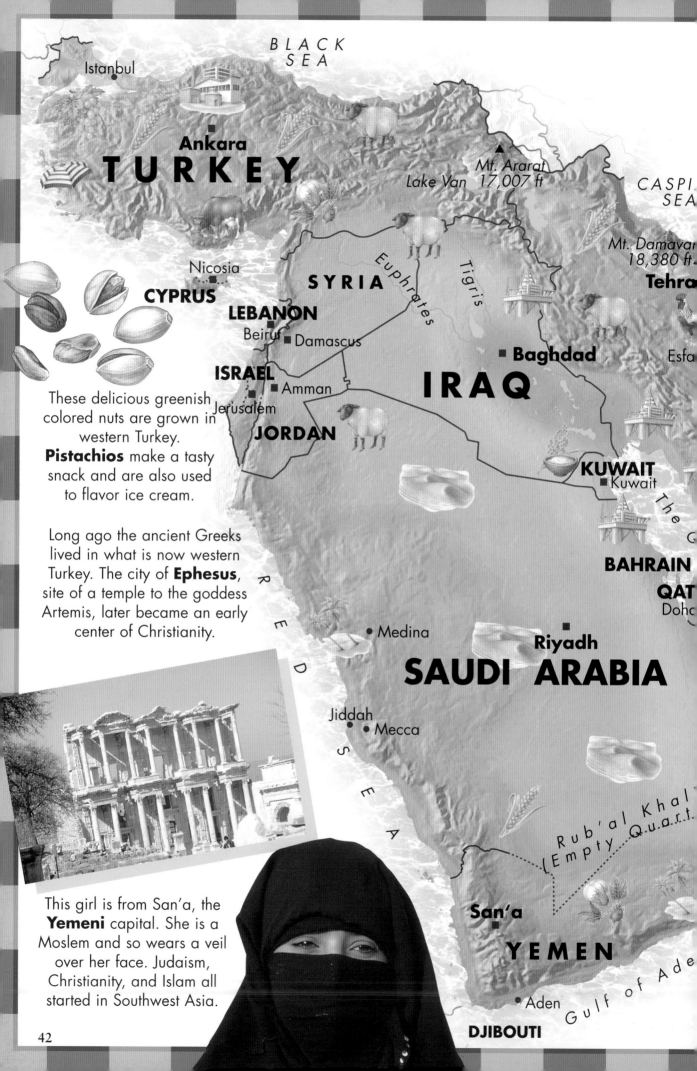

BLACK SEA

Istanbul

Ankara
T U R K E Y

Mt. Ararat 17,007 ft
Lake Van

CASPIAN SEA

Mt. Damavar 18,380 ft.

Nicosia

CYPRUS

S Y R I A

Euphrates

Tigris

Tehra

LEBANON
Beirut • Damascus

ISRAEL
• Amman

Jerusalem

JORDAN

Baghdad

I R A Q

Esfa

These delicious greenish colored nuts are grown in western Turkey. **Pistachios** make a tasty snack and are also used to flavor ice cream.

KUWAIT
• Kuwait

Long ago the ancient Greeks lived in what is now western Turkey. The city of **Ephesus**, site of a temple to the goddess Artemis, later became an early center of Christianity.

R
E
D

The G

BAHRAIN

QAT
Doha

• Medina

Riyadh

SAUDI ARABIA

Jiddah
• Mecca

S
E
A

Rub' al Khal (Empty Quart

This girl is from San'a, the **Yemeni** capital. She is a Moslem and so wears a veil over her face. Judaism, Christianity, and Islam all started in Southwest Asia.

• San'a

Y E M E N

• Aden

Gulf of Ade

42

DJIBOUTI

Southwest Asia

This region of Asia is often called the Near East or the Middle East. Its western parts border the Mediterranean Sea. These have a gentle, warm climate, which makes it possible to grow fruits such as oranges and lemons. The Arabian peninsula is the land surrounded by the Red Sea, the Indian Ocean, and the Persian Gulf. It is occupied by Jordan, Saudi Arabia, and the small countries of Yemen, Oman, United Arab Emirates (UAE), Qatar, Bahrain, and Kuwait. This a land of hot, sandy deserts. Little can grow here, but it is rich in oil and natural gas.

Eastern Syria and Iraq are also desert regions, but these are crossed by the rivers Tigris and Euphrates. It was here that the world's first farmers founded towns and cities thousands of years ago. Eastern Turkey and northern Iran include mountains, windswept plains and rolling grasslands, which are very cold in winter. Iran also has ranges of mountains and deserts.

Mashhad

IRAN

Abu Dhabi

Gulf of Oman

UNITED ARAB EMIRATES

Muscat

OMAN

Socotra (YEMEN)

These towers in **Kuwait** are used to take the salt out of seawater, so that it can be drunk or used on the land.

This camel rider is one of the **Bedouin**, a nomadic people of the region. Camels are the ideal transport for desert areas.

Beautiful **pearls** form in oysters in the warm seas of Southwest Asia. They are very valuable.

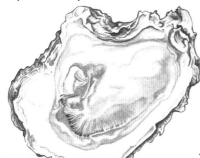

India and its Neighbors

Mount Everest is the highest mountain on Earth. It lies on the border between Nepal and Tibet, in the Himalaya range.

Colorful, sparkling costumes are worn by these **Indian dancers**. India is famous for its richly colored silks and cottons and its silver jewelry.

This mass of land is so big that it is sometimes called the Indian subcontinent, or simply the subcontinent. It is separated from Central Asia by the world's biggest mountains, which are in the Himalaya and Karakoram ranges. These climb to 29,028 feet above sea level at Mount Everest. Snowy peaks stretch all the way from eastern Afghanistan, through northern Pakistan and India to Nepal and Bhutan.

To the south are the wide, dusty plains of India, crossed by the Ganges. In Bangladesh, this river splits into many channels before flowing into the Bay of Bengal. India is a country of deserts, forested hills, small villages, and large bustling cities. The climate is mostly tropical and very hot, with monsoon winds bringing heavy summer rainstorms. In the far south is the tropical island nation of Sri Lanka.

The region produces wheat, tea, sugarcane, rice, jute, and cotton. It includes the sites of ancient civilizations and places which are holy to Hindus, Buddhists, Sikhs, and Muslims.

AFGHANISTAN

Kabul

Khyber Pass

PAKISTAN

Islamabad

Lahore

Indus

NEPAL

Delhi

New Delhi

HIMA

INDIA

Coriander

Ground turmeric

Andaman & Nicobar Is. (India)

Ginger

Indian food includes delicious curries, chutneys, rice, and vegetable dishes. They are cooked with different **kinds of spice.**

This **Bengal tiger** has become very rare. It is protected in special reserves in India, Bangladesh, and Nepal.

Brahmaputra

■ Dhaka

Ganges

Calcutta

BAY OF BENGAL

Ahmadabad

•Surat

Nagpur

Godavari

Mumbai (Bombay)

Pune

Hyderabad

•Chennai (Madras)

Bangalore

SRI LANKA

Colombo ■

•Galle

INDIAN OCEAN

A woman picks **tea** in the green hills of Sri Lanka. This small island nation to the south of India is the biggest exporter of tea in the world.

ARABIAN SEA

MALDIVES

Many people say that the **Taj Mahal,** a marble tomb, is the most beautiful building in the world. It was built near Agra in India by a Muslim emperor named Shah Jahan, who ruled from 1627 to 1666.

45

China and its Neighbors

China covers an area about the size of western Europe. It is ringed by high mountains, empty deserts, and tropical seas where fierce storms called typhoons are common.

Most people live in the fertile eastern part of the country, which is crossed by great rivers such as the Huang He and the Chang Jiang. More people live in China than in any other country in the world. Chinese farmers grow rice, tea, wheat, and corn. China is the center of a very ancient civilization and was famous in history for its pottery and fine silk.

The Mongols live in a northern part of China and also in the rolling grasslands and deserts of Mongolia itself. The Koreans live to the northeast, on a peninsula containing North and South Korea.

KAZAKHSTAN

MONGOLI

Ürümqi

TAKLIMAKAN DESERT

CHINA

INDIA

PLATEAU OF TIBET

HIMALAYA

Lhasa

Mt. Everest▲ 29,029 ft

So

Qin Shi Huangdi was the first emperor of China. When he died in 210BC his tomb was surrounded by a **buried army**. This was made up of thousands of life-sized soldiers, made of clay.

Traditional wooden sailing boats called **junks** may still be seen among the more modern ships around the coasts of China.

Many **Mongols** follow their herds of sheep on horseback. They live in a round felt tent known as a **ger** or **yurt**.

There are many different styles of Chinese cooking, from Beijing in the north to Guangzhou in the south. Rice, noodles, and dumplings are popular, steamed in **bamboo containers**.

Hong Kong is a small, crowded piece of land in southern China. It was mostly ruled by Britain from 1842 until 1997. It is a center of business and tourism.

Farm workers in China plant out **rice** seedlings in a flooded paddy. China has so many people to feed that every possible bit of spare land is used to grow crops. Rice is served with most meals.

RUSSIA

Amur

Harbin

Ulan Bator

GOBI DESERT

Shenyang

NORTH KOREA

P'yongyang

Dalian

Seoul

SOUTH KOREA

Beijing

Tianjin

Zibo

YELLOW SEA

Taiyuan

Huang He

EAST CHINA SEA

Lanzhou

ang He

Xi'an

Nanjing

Shanghai

Chengdu

Wuhan

Chongqing

Fuzhou

Taipei

TAIWAN

Kunming

Guangzhou

Hong Kong

MACAO

Hainan

Japan

Kuril Is.
[Russia]

H O K K A I D O

▲ Asahi Mt.
7,511 ft

Sapporo

Kita

The Japanese capital is **Tokyo**. It is a center of business and industry and merges with another great city, the port of Yokohama. It has suffered in the past from severe earthquakes.

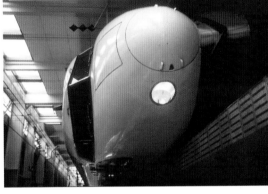

The high-speed **Bullet Train** has become a symbol of modern Japan. Japan's islands are linked by some of the world's longest and most modern bridges and tunnels.

Thousands of small islands lie to the east of China on the edge of the Pacific Ocean. They make up a country called Japan. There are four main islands—Hokkaido, Honshu, Shikoku, and Kyushu. These are mostly very mountainous, so the big cities have spread along the strips of flat land around the coast. This is where most of the good farmland is sited, too. Japan produces rice and tea, and has a large fishing fleet. The north of the country is cold and snowy in winter, but the south has a warm, tropical climate.

Japan has very few resources such as oil or coal. Even so, it is a very modern country which has many big businesses and produces cars and electrical goods. At the same time Japan is an ancient country, with many traditional customs and ceremonies. You can still see beautiful Buddhist temples and castles too, dating back to the Middle Ages. Japan has long been famous for its beautiful art, architecture, and pottery. Japanese artists carry on these traditions in modern dance, films, and even in

JAPAN

Mount Fuji are covered in snow. Japanese artists have painted this beautiful volcano many times.

The slopes of

Traditional dress is still worn in Japan on many special occasions. This woman wears sandals and a silk gown called a kimono.

Sumo wrestlers weigh in at about 300 pounds. Their aim is to topple their opponent or throw them out of the ring. The match starts with long ceremonies, but the action is normally over very quickly.

Favorite Japanese foods include rice, fish, prawns, seaweed, pork, bean curd, and noodles. These are traditionally eaten with chopsticks.

Sendai

Mito

HONSHU

Tokyo

Yokohama

Mt. Fuji 12,385 ft

PACIFIC OCEAN

Nagoya

Kyoto

Osaka

Kobe

Kii Channel

SHIKOKU

Hiroshima

Kitakyushu

Fukuoka

KYUSHU

49

Southeast Asia

The southeast of the Asian continent borders India and China. It is a land of flooded ricefields, forests, remote hill country, and great rivers, such as the Irrawaddy and the Mekong. This region has beautiful Buddhist temples and ruins left behind by ancient civilizations. Sadly, it has also seen terrible wars in the last 50 years, while in some areas the traditional way of life has been completely changed by tourism or, in the cities of Singapore or Kuala Lumpur, by big business.

The mainland states include Myanmar, Thailand, Cambodia, Laos, and Vietnam. Malaysia takes up part of the mainland but also most of the forested, tropical island of Borneo. The small state of Brunei is in the north of Borneo. The south of the region is occupied by the long chains of islands which make up Indonesia. In the far east, bordering the Pacific Ocean, are the Philippines.

INDIA

MYANMAR (BURMA)

CHINA

Yangon (Rangoon)

Han

LAOS

Vientiane

THAILAN

Bangkok

CAMBO

Phnom Penh

Ho C
Minh C

Gulf of
Thailand

Strait of Malacca

M A L

Medan

Kuala Lun

Sumatra

SINGAPO

Jaka

People of both Indian and Chinese descent live in the city of **Singapore** and their styles of cooking have mingled—deliciously!

This ornate stone demon guards the royal palace in **Bangkok**, capital of Thailand.

The **orangutan** lives in the rain forests of Borneo and Sumatra. Throughout Southeast Asia forests are threatened by logging, clearance, and fires.

ETNAM

A boat is anchored by the banks of the Hue river, in northeastern **Vietnam**. Cone-shaped straw hats protect the wearer from tropical sun and monsoon rains.

Luzon

■Manila

PHILIPPINES

While most Indonesians are Muslims, the **Balinese** are Hindus. The island of Bali has many beautiful old temples and palaces, where dances like this can be seen.

SULU SEA

Mindanao

Bandar Seri Begawan

A SIA   **BRUNEI**

CELEBES SEA

BORNEO

Moluccas

Sulawesi

I N D O N E S I A

NEW GUINEA

AVA   *SEA*   *BANDA SEA*

FLORES SEA

va   •Surabaya

Lombok

Bali

Sumba   *Timor*

Singapore is a tiny independent country. Most of it is taken up by the city of Singapore, an international center of business and trade.

Meet the **komodo dragon**, the world's biggest lizard. It lives only on Komodo and a few neighboring islands in Indonesia.

North and West Africa

The Mediterranean coast has a pleasant, warm climate. To the south, beyond the Atlas mountains, is the world's largest desert, the Sahara. Its burning hot sands and rocks stretch all the way from Mauritania to Egypt. The River Nile, the world's longest river, meets the sea in Egypt after a long journey northward across Sudan. It rises in the mountains of Central Africa and Ethiopia.

The countries bordering the southern edge of the Sahara make up the Sahel. This is a dry, dusty region where thin grass is grazed by cattle and goats. Nearer the coast, on the Gulf of Guinea, there is fertile farmland, forest and the oil-rich lands around the River Niger. West Africa produces peanuts, cocoa, palm oil, and cotton.

Peoples of the north include Berbers and Arabs. The many different peoples living to the south of the Sahara are mostly Black Africans. Religions of the region include Islam, Christianity, and spirit religions.

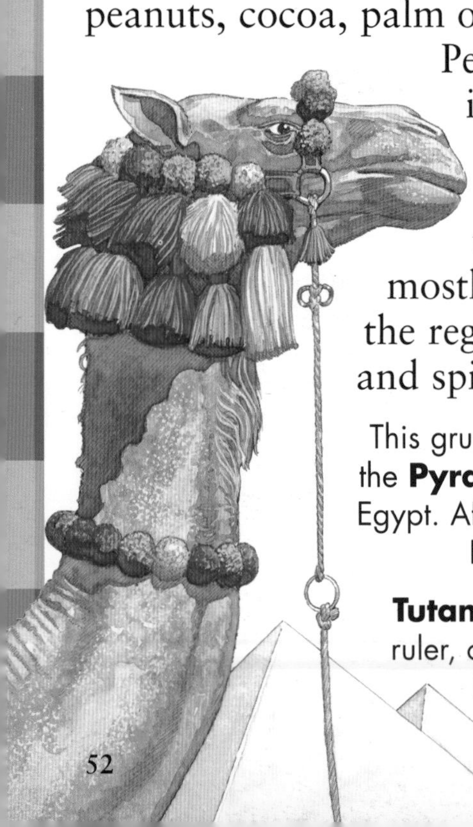

This grumpy-looking camel is looking out over the **Pyramids**, the royal burial sites of ancient Egypt. Africa's first great civilization grew up in Egypt about 5,000 years ago.

Tutankhamun died in 1327BC. He was ruler, or pharaoh, of ancient Egypt and was buried with all sorts of rich treasures.

Map labels: Strait of Gibra, Madeira, Rabat, Casablanca, MOROCCO, ATLAS MTS., CANARY ISLANDS, ALGE, Western Sahara, S, A, Cape Blanc, MAURITANIA, MALI, Nouakchott, Timbuktu, Niger, Dakar, SENEGAL, Banjul, GAMBIA, Nic, Ouagadougou, Bissau, Bamako, BURKINA FA, GUINEA-BISSAU, GUINEA, Conakry, Freetown, SIERRA LEONE, IVORY COAST, GHANA, TOGO, Monrovia, Yamoussoukro, Lomé, LIBERIA, Abidjan, Accra

Africa's Mediterranean coast was once part of the mighty Roman empire. **Roman ruins** can be seen in Tunisia and Libya.

Most North Africans are **Muslims**, but in southern regions there are many Christians.

iers
■ Tunis

TUNISIA

Tripoli
● Ghadamis

LIBYA

H A R A

HAGGAR MTS.

TIBESTI MTS.

Alexandria ● Port Said
■ ● Suez
QATTARA Cairo
DEPRESSION

EGYPT

Lake Nasser

R E D   S E A

Women take turns to **pound grain**, in this traditional way of making flour in West Africa.

Port Sudan

NIGER

CHAD

Lake Chad

Kano

■ N'Djaména

■ Abuja

SUDAN

Khartoum ■

Nile
Atbara
Blue Nile
Lake Tana

ERITREA
■ Asmara

DJIBOUTI
■ Djibouti

Addis Ababa

ETHIOPIA

NIGERIA
CAMEROON
■ Yaoundé

Malabo
EQUATORIAL GUINEA

CENTRAL AFRICAN REPUBLIC

White Nile

UGANDA

KENYA

SOMALIA

This **water carrier** is selling drinks of cool, fresh water on the hot streets of Marrakesh, in Morocco.

In **Burkina Faso** a donkey pulls a cartload of hay. Droughts are common in the Sahel region and food for cattle is very valuable.

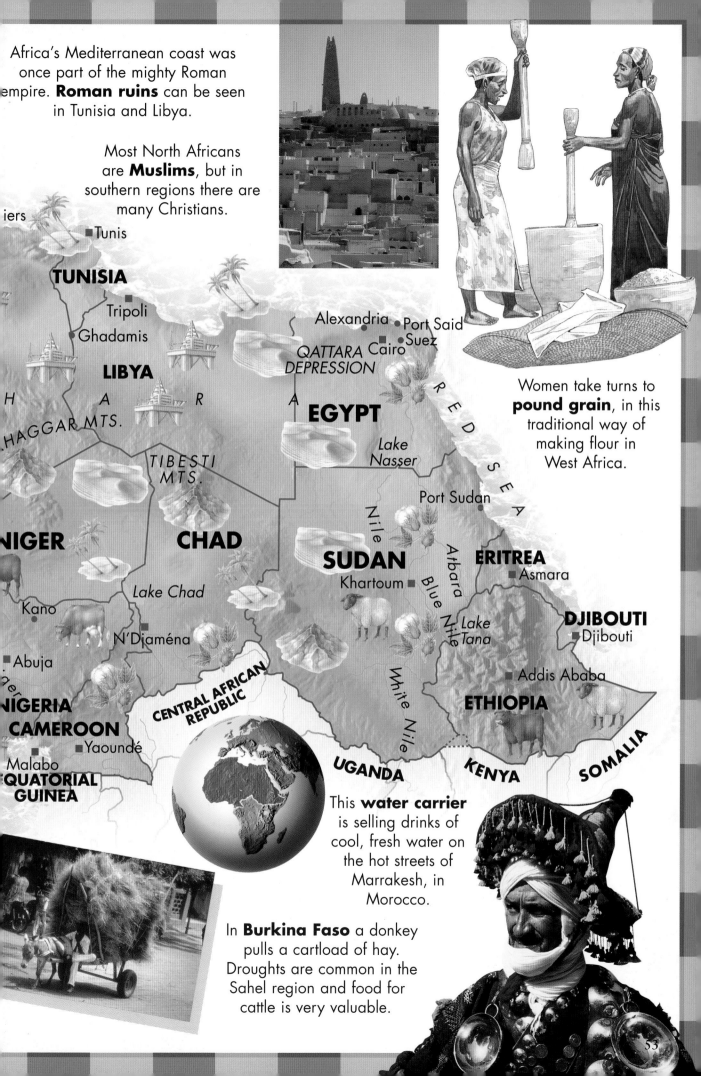

53

Central, Eastern, and Southern Africa

Central Africa is a land of rain forests, crossed by the River Congo. To the south are the Kalahari and Namib deserts, and the mountains and grasslands of South Africa. The east of the continent is divided by the Great Rift Valley, a network of deep cracks in the Earth's surface. It is fringed by volcanoes and in places has filled with water to form long lakes. East Africa includes rich farmland, which produces tobacco, fruit, and vegetables. There are wide grassy plains dotted with thorny trees, grazed by great herds of wild animals including zebra, giraffe and many types of antelope. The continent is bordered by the Atlantic to the west and by the Indian Ocean to the east. Madagascar is Africa's largest island.

The **Masai people** live in southern Kenya and northern Tanzania. Many of them herd cattle.

SÃO TOMÉ & PRÍNCIPE

Boz

Libreville **REP. CON**

GABON

Brazzav

Kinsh

Cabinda (ANGOLA)

Luanda

A N

Vast herds of wild animals still roam eastern and southern Africa. They include lion, antelope, **elephant,** and rhinoceros.

NAMIB DESERT

Windh

Wind shapes the shifiting sands of the **Namib desert** in southwestern Africa. This harsh, dry region borders the Atlantic coast for 800 miles.

Sorghum is a grain crop much like corn which thrives in the hot and dry conditions of Zimbabwe.

Cape T

Cape Good

The **Zulus** are the largest group of peoples living in South Africa. Many different peoples live in the region, each with their own language and traditions.

The River Zambezi forms **Victoria Falls,** a huge waterfall, between Zambia and Zimbabwe. Its local name is Mose-la-Tunya, the "smoke that thunders".

SOMALIA

ENTRAL
FRICAN
EPUBLIC
Bangassou
ngui

Ue/e

ongo

UGANDA

KENYA

Mogadishu

Kampala
RWANDA
Kigali
Lake
Victoria
Nairobi

.MOCRATIC REP.
OF CONGO

BURUNDI

Kananga

Sankuru

Kasai

Lake
Tanganyika

Kilimanjaro
19,335 ft
Dodoma

SEYCHELLES

INDIAN OCEAN

TANZANIA

Lake Malawi
(Nyasa)

COMOROS

MALAWI
Lilongwe

Moçambique

A

ZAMBIA

Lusaka
Zambezi
Blantyre

MOZAMBIQUE

Mozambique Channel

MAURITIUS

Harare

ZIMBABWE

AMIBIA

Antananarivo

Limpopo

MADAGASCAR

BOTSWANA
Gaborone
*ALAHARI
DESERT*
Pretoria
Maputo

Mbabane

SWAZILAND
Maseru

OUTH
FRICA

LESOTHO

This animal is a ring-tailed **lemur**. Lemurs are only found on the island of Madagascar. They live in forest and dry scrub land, where they eat fruit and insects.

Australia

The center of Australia is an empty wilderness of desert, rocks, and scrub. It is bordered by grasslands, tropical forests and creeks. In the east are the mountains of the Great Dividing Range. The chief rivers are the Murray and the Darling, in the southeast. The remote country regions of Australia are known as the "outback." They are grazed by huge herds of sheep and cattle, and in places are worked by mining companies.

Most Australians live in the big cities around the coast, such as Brisbane, Sydney, Melbourne, Adelaide, and Perth. Across Bass Strait is the island of Tasmania, which has a cooler climate.

Today's Australians include the first inhabitants of the land, the Aborigines, as well as the descendants of British people who seized their lands about 200 years ago. There are also many people from other European countries and from Asia.

Sydney Opera House rises from Sydney Harbor like a giant sailing ship.

A **giant clam** lies in the tropical waters of this 1,200 mile-long bank of coral.

GRE
SAND
DESE

GIBS
DESE

WESTERN AUSTRALIA

GREA
VICTO.
DESE

Perth

Archipelago of Recherche

Through the surf **rowers** break white water during a beach contest. Australia is famous for its surf.

The **kookaburra** is a common Australian bird. It has a loud cackling call which gives it the nickname of the laughing jackass.

Surfers' Paradise is one of many resorts built along the eastern coast of Australia. Sunshine and surf attract many visitors.

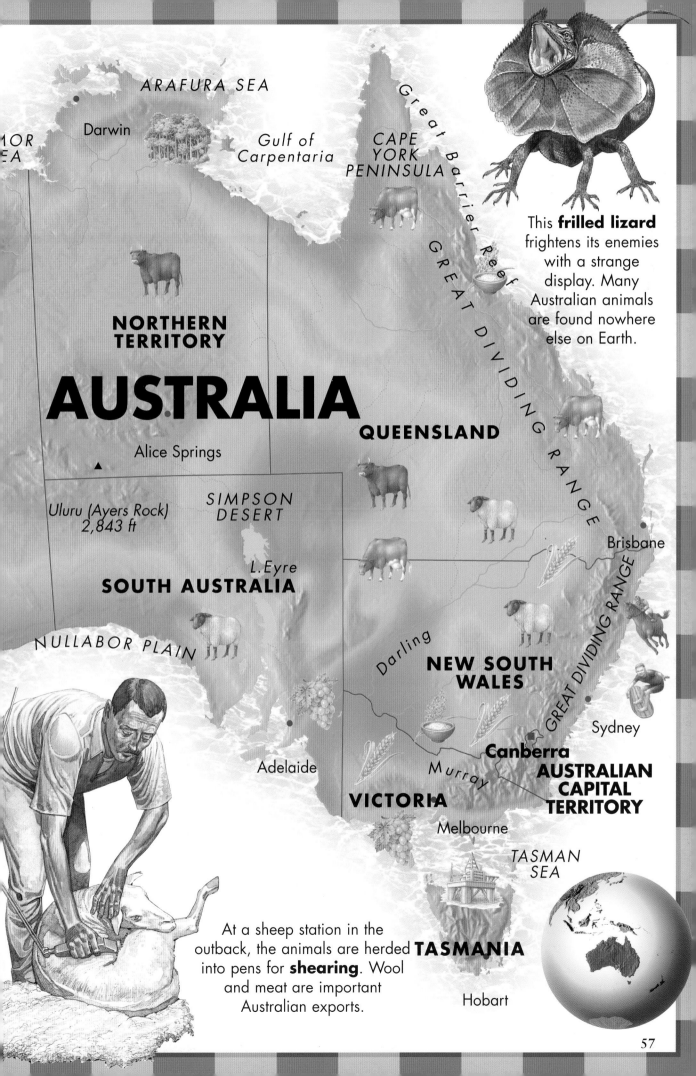

ARAFURA SEA

Darwin

Gulf of
Carpentaria

CAPE
YORK
PENINSULA

Great Barrier Reef

This **frilled lizard** frightens its enemies with a strange display. Many Australian animals are found nowhere else on Earth.

NORTHERN
TERRITORY

AUSTRALIA

QUEENSLAND

Alice Springs

GREAT DIVIDING RANGE

Uluru (Ayers Rock)
2,843 ft

SIMPSON
DESERT

L. Eyre

SOUTH AUSTRALIA

NULLABOR PLAIN

Darling

NEW SOUTH
WALES

GREAT DIVIDING RANGE

Brisbane

Sydney

Canberra
AUSTRALIAN
CAPITAL
TERRITORY

Adelaide

Murray

VICTORIA

Melbourne

TASMAN
SEA

At a sheep station in the outback, the animals are herded into pens for **shearing**. Wool and meat are important Australian exports.

TASMANIA

Hobart

MOR
EA

New Zealand and the Pacific

If you sail eastward from Australia, you reach a group of islands about 1,000 miles out into the Pacific Ocean. They make up a country called New Zealand. There are two main islands, North and South. They include high mountains and glaciers, hot springs, gushing spouts called geysers, and grassy plains. The Maori people were the first people to settle these islands, followed after the 1800s by Europeans, especially the British. New Zealand raises sheep and exports dairy products, fruit, and meat.

The Pacific is the world's biggest ocean stretching all the way to the Americas. It is dotted with small islands, and these are home to three main groups of people—the Polynesians (who include the Maoris), the Micronesians, and the Melanesians. They live by fishing, growing crops such as coconuts and yams, by mining and by tourism.

Yellow Sea

East China Sea

SOUTH CHINA SEA

Philippine Sea

Northern Mariana Islands (USA)

Guam

Federated States of Micronesia

Palau

Celebes Sea

Papua New Guinea

Solomon Islands

Coral Sea

Papua New Guinea is made up of many islands. Some small islands are surrounded by shallow reefs.

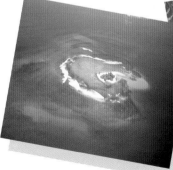

This is a market in **Vanuatu,** a Pacific nation made up of 80 islands. They produce cocoa, dried coconut, and bananas.

The **Kiwi** is a flightless bird which comes out by night to search for insects on the forest floor. It is the national emblem of New Zealand.

This **Karawari woman** from Papua New Guinea has painted her face for a traditional tribal gathering.

BERING SEA

Giant tortoises live on the Galapagos Islands. In fact the islands' name means "tortoises" in Spanish. These Pacific Islands are governed by the South American country of Ecuador.

South Island, New Zealand, has snowfields, glaciers and **high mountains**. Mount Cook reaches 12,395 feet above sea level.

NORTH PACIFIC OCEAN

Midway Island (USA)

Wake Island (USA)

Hawaii (USA)

Marshall Islands

The brown nut of the **coconut**, with its white center, is found inside a large green fruit. Coconuts are a valuable Pacific island export.

Nauru

Kiribati

Tuvalu

Vanuatu

Samoa

American Samoa

Fiji

New Caledonia (France)

Tonga

Cook Islands (New Zealand)

Galapagos (Ecuador)

Auckland

Waikato

Hamilton

Rotorua

L. Taupo

▲ *Ruapehu 2,797m*

Napier

Hastings

Palmerston North

■ **Wellington**

Huge stone heads were carved by Polynesian settlers on **Easter Island**, about 1,000 years ago.

NEW ZEALAND

Kaibola canoes are the traditional means of transport of the Pacific Islands. This crew is from Papua New Guinea.

Mt.Cook 3,764m▲

SOUTHERN ALPS

Cook Strait

Christchurch

This fine **wooden carving** was placed above the door of a Moari building.

Clutha

Dunedin

Invercargill

Stewart Island

Traditionally, **Maoris** wore cloaks and tattooed their faces. Maoris today retain many customs.

Polar Lands

The northern part of the globe is called the Arctic. It takes in the northern parts of North America, Europe and Asia. These are lands of ice and snow and deep-frozen treeless soil, called tundra. They surround the Arctic Ocean, of which large areas are permanently capped in thick ice. At the center of this ice cap is the northernmost point on Earth, the North Pole.

Peoples of the Arctic include the Inuit of Greenland and Canada, the Saami of Scandinavia, and the many peoples from the north of the Russian Federation, such as the Chukchi, Yupigyts, Evenks, and Samoyeds. Some live by hunting and fishing, some by herding reindeer, and some in more recent Arctic industries, such as oil and mining. The Arctic Ocean supports fish, whales, walrus, and seals.

The **Inuit people** live in Canada and Greenland. Traditionally their hunters made overnight camps out of blocks of frozen snow. These were shaped into domes.

BERING SEA

ALASKA (USA)

Mackenzie

New Siberian Islands

Lena

ARCTIC OCEAN

CANADA

Victoria Island

North Magnetic Pole

★ North Pole

Yenis

Ellesmere Island

Franz Josef Land

Novaya Zemlya

KARA SEA

GREENLAND (DENMARK)

Svalbard (Norway)

Murmansk

Archangel

ICELAND

Polar bears hunt seals on the ice.

The **Snowy owl** lives in Arctic regions.

Teams of dogs known as huskies, pull sleds across the snow in Antarctica.

The southernmost point on the globe is called the South Pole. It is surrounded by Antarctica, the coldest and windiest land on Earth. This is a land of mountains and dazzling white icefields, split by deep cracks called crevasses. Large areas of frozen sea surround the land. Massive slabs of ice break off in spring to form icebergs. No people have ever settled in Antarctica, but there are scientific bases. Some countries claim parts of Antarctica and there may be rich minerals in the rocks deep beneath the ice. However, many people think that Antarctica should be left alone, as the last real wilderness on our planet.

The southern part of the world has its winter while the northern part has summer. Polar regions stay dark for the whole day at midwinter, and stay light during the night at midsummer.

Walruses are big blubbery animals with flippers and long tusks, which they use to scrape clams off the seabed. They swim in bitterly cold Arctic waters.

Ships entering **polar waters** must be strengthened so that they can smash their way through floating ice.

The big tails of **whales** are called flukes. Many kinds of whale come to feed in polar waters.

Emperor penguins are Antarctic birds. They cannot fly, but they are excellent swimmers.

Many different kinds of **seal** breed in polar waters. They gather in large numbers on rocks, ice floes, and beaches.

Up to nine tenths of an **iceberg** may be under water. They are a hazard to shipping.

ATLANTIC OCEAN
Permanent Extent of Sea Ice
INDIAN OCEAN
Drake Passage
WEDELL SEA
Coats Land
Maud Land
Enderby Land
Antarctic Peninsula
Ronne Ice Shelf
Cape Darnley
South Pole
GREATER ANTARCTICA
Vinson Massif ▲ 17,744 ft
TRANSANTARCTIC MTNS.
LESSER ANTARCTICA
Wilkes Land
Ross Ice Shelf
Erebus 12,444 ft
ROSS SEA
PACIFIC OCEAN

Index

Acknowledgments

The publishers wish to thank the artists who have contributed to this book:
Martin Camm, John James, Gill Platt, Terry Riley, Peter Sarson, Roger Smith, Mike White, Alison Winfield

All photographs used in the First Atlas are from MKP Archives